37444000128352

S0-AJN-201

Lightning will usually strike the tallest object

$\mathcal{L}$ightning

Jill Kalz

A⁺
Smart Apple Media

COPYRIGHT

⌇ Published by Smart Apple Media

1980 Lookout Drive, North Mankato, MN 56003

Designed by Rita Marshall

Copyright © 2003 Smart Apple Media. International copyright reserved in all countries. No part of this book may be reproduced in any form without written permission from the publisher.

Printed in the United States of America

⌇ Photographs by JLM Visuals (Doug Reid), Library of Congress, Tom Stack & Associates (Spencer Swanger, William L. Wantland), Weatherstock (Warren Faidley)

⌇ Library of Congress Cataloging-in-Publication Data

Kalz, Jill. Lightning / by Jill Kalz. p. cm. — (Weather)

Includes bibliographical references and index.

Summary: Discusses the nature, effects, and potential danger of lightning.

⌇ ISBN 1-58340-154-7

1. Lightning—Juvenile literature. [1. Lightning.] I. Title. II. Weather (Smart Apple Media).

QC966.5 .K345 2002   551.56'32—dc21   2001049979

⌇ First Edition 9 8 7 6 5 4 3 2 1

A Giant Spark

The sky blackened and the wind howled. Bright flashes of light lit the insides of the clouds. Certainly not good weather for flying a kite! But one man thought differently. As the rain soaked his clothes, he flew a kite high into the clouds. A metal key dangled from the kite string. It was 1752, and the man's name was Benjamin Franklin. Franklin believed that lightning was nothing more than a giant spark of **electricity**. When lightning struck his kite and sparks jumped

Benjamin Franklin proved that lightning is electricity

from the key, Franklin knew he was right. 〰 Before this

discovery, many people believed that lightning was created by

the gods. Northern Europeans once believed that Thor, the

god of thunder, created lightning storms **Lightning hap-**

pens all over the

by blowing through his wild, red beard. **world; it strikes**

the earth an

When he was angry, he roared, and **average of 100**

times every

thunder rolled from the skies. Ancient **second.**

Greeks told of one-eyed giants who hammered lightning bolts

for Zeus, the king of the gods, to throw at his enemies.

Lightning is created inside cumulonimbus clouds

Lightning's white light can appear colored from a distance

Birth of a Bolt

Most thunderstorms happen during the summer. The sun's heat causes large amounts of water to **evaporate**.

This warm water vapor, or gas, rises quickly into the air. As it gets higher, it cools, changes into water droplets, and forms a cloud. Each water droplet in a cloud carries a tiny bit of electricity. As more moisture collects, the cloud grows bigger, and the amount of electricity

The energy in an average flash of lightning could light a 100-watt light bulb for three months.

Clouds are full of the electricity that causes lightning

increases. There are two kinds of electricity: positive charges and negative charges. The **attraction** between these two charges causes lightning. Most lightning happens within or between giant cumulonimbus clouds. Sometimes it strikes the ground, but no one knows exactly where it will strike. When lightning strikes, it looks like one giant bolt, but it is really a set of **strokes**, bouncing back and forth. Each stroke is about the width of a pencil. A thin "leader" stroke hits the earth first, followed by a powerful

The top of the Empire State Building in New York City is hit by lightning about 25 times each year.

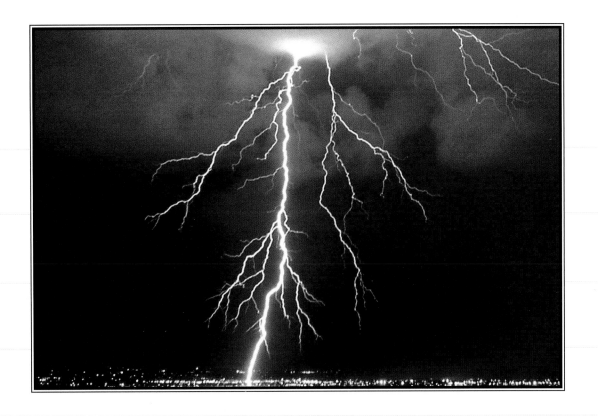

"return" stroke. This stroke is so fast that a rocket traveling

at the same speed would reach the moon in just two and a

half seconds!

Lightning can light up the night sky during storms

Lightning's Partner

Lightning can instantly heat the air in its path to an incredible 54,000 °F (30,000 °C). That is five times hotter than the sun! When air heats up quickly, it explodes or bangs. Thunder is the booming sound created by the super-heated air in lightning's path.

Lightning flashes can stretch up to a dozen miles (19 km) from their source and strike out of a clear, blue sky.

Lightning and thunder happen at the same time, but light travels much faster than sound. This means that lightning is seen before thunder is heard. You can tell how far away a

storm is by counting the number of seconds between the flash

and the boom. The number of seconds divided by five will

give you the distance in miles (divide by three for kilometers).

Lightning often splits or forks into many branches

Safety Tips

Lightning is always dangerous. It can split trees or start fires. It can melt metal. Each year, lightning kills more people in the United States than hurricanes or tornadoes. But if you know how to stay safe, you will have nothing to fear.

If you are outside and hear thunder, go inside. Being in a car is safer than being in the open air, but the safest place to be during a thunderstorm is inside a house. Turn off the television and computer and do not use the telephone. Lightning moves easily through water, so stay away from the

shower, tub, and sink. ～ If you cannot go inside, stay away

from water and trees. Avoid high places and large, open spaces.

Lightning will strike the tallest object it can find. Do not let it

No one can tell where a lightning bolt will strike

be you! Find a low place far from any metal. Squat down, tuck your head, and cover your ears with your hands. If lightning is nearby, your hair may stand on end and your skin may tingle.

Lightning is powerful, but it can also be beautiful. It stretches across the dark sky like bright, skinny fingers. It zigzags, splits, and jumps. It flashes inside clouds like white fireworks. Watching lightning storms from a safe place can be exciting, but remember to cover your ears! Wherever lightning goes, thunder is never very far behind.

A photograph of lightning painted different colors

Making Sparks

If you have ever shuffled your feet on carpet and then touched a metal doorknob, you have created static electricity. This activity will show you another way to make sparks. Be sure to have an adult help you. For best results, do this activity in a darkened room.

What You Need

A plastic tablecloth   Tape

A metal bowl   A rubber glove

A fork

What You Do

1. Tape the tablecloth to a counter or table so it does not move.

2. Hold the metal bowl with a gloved hand. Now rub the bowl against the cloth for a few minutes.

3. With your ungloved hand, bring the fork close to the bowl but do not touch it. Do you see the spark jump between the bowl and the fork? Can you hear a tiny crackle? You have just made your own "mini-lightning!"

Static electricity can make your hair stand on end

Index

Words to Know

attraction (uh-TRAK-shun)—a force that pulls two objects together, such as the attraction between magnets

cumulonimbus (kewm-u-low-NIM-bus)—huge, flat-topped storm clouds, also known as thunderheads

electricity (ee-lek-TRI-seh-tee)—a form of energy created by the movement of positively and negatively charged particles

evaporate (ee-VAP-uh-rate)—to change from a liquid to a gas

strokes (STROHKS)—blows or blasts that are repeated

Read More

Branley, Franklyn M. *Flash, Crash, Rumble, and Roll*. New York: HarperCollins Publishers, 1999.

Burby, Liza N. *Electrical Storms*. New York: Rosen Publishing Group, 1999.

Kramer, Stephen. *Lightning*. Minneapolis, Minn.: Carolrhoda Books, 1992.

Internet Sites

FEMA for Kids: Thunderstorms
http://www.fema.gov/kids/thunder.htm

Kids' Lightning Information and Safety
http://www.azstarnet.com/anubis/zaphome.htm

National Weather Service: Lightning Safety
http://www.lightningsafety.noaa.gov